HOSTJANE

HostJane

Tiger Economy of Freelance Marketplaces

JULIANNA ROBBINS

Sourcebook Guides

CONTENTS

~ 1 ~

The Economic Uncertainty of Marketplaces

1

~ 2 ~

Airtasker - A Canary in the Coal Mine

7

~ 3 ~

A Host Turned Marketplace

10

~ 4 ~

References

12

~ 1 ~

THE ECONOMIC UNCERTAINTY OF MARKETPLACES

The "gig economy" isn't typically associated with worker exploitation. To most people, the *gig economy* is a phrase coined to denote an industry where workers can increase their auxiliary income streams on weekly or monthly basis by facilitating a 'side hustle'. Gig platforms aren't documented on case law databases like LexiNexis nor have there been any legal precedents or anti-trust lawsuits such as United States v. Microsoft Corporation, 253 F.3d 34 (D.C. Cir. 2001 LexisNexis) where government intervened to protect free market competition in the gig economy space. Nevertheless, the Economic Policy Institute, a legal think tank based in Washington D.C. is considering the macroeconomic question whether Americans 'side hustle'—which according to McKinsey's American Opportunity Survey (AOS) involves 36% of the U.S. workforce—has in itself come to be dominated by a handful of gig platforms such as DoorDash, 99designs and TaskRabbit who are not adding reciprocal value but gatekeeping individual freelancers' sales routes to final consumers, to fulfill monopsonist conditions to exploit workers.

The ease to replacing a second offline job with virtual work offerings, billed in promotional literature of better known multinational gig platforms, such as Fiverr, eBay, and Upwork (and Uber

Eats in the food delivery space) who all seek to attract and retain talent is, on terms of Deci and Ryan's 2000 Self-Determination Theory (SDT), not at all easy and what motivates freelancer behavior to sign up, and buyer loyalty, carries a much higher cost burden to the individual worker.

To put it another way, American freelancers are no longer as free as they were 10 years ago to earn a 'side hustle' or regular weekly gig income because the gig economy has been changed by a handful of multinationals platform whose business models rely on millions of freelancers vying for sales in an increasingly low oxygen overpopulated pool. The result is a more static, authoritarian stranglehold that has replaced free market variables with systemic control, with a few shareholders affecting the incomes of many disassociated, individual freelancers and small startups attempting to acquire new business using these large platforms - with little to no choice and no alternatives.

"Market leaders" have effectively skewed the vertical market to become the only place for freelancers to sell online, and en route to this new destination, many of these platforms are owned by the same shareholders.

"Work Your Way. You bring the skill. We'll make earning easy," Fiverr tells college graduates looking for an interim job to meet rent payments. "Drive when you want, make what you need. Earn on your own schedule," reads Uber's website, which is inundated by new driver sign ups every time the economy contracts and threatens to enter a recession. With the exception of Airbnb, San Francisco, CA-based data analytics firm Priceonomics says the "majority of workers at Etsy, Uber, Fiverr fall into the $100 or under per month bracket". For years minimum wages in labor laws and the presence of labor unions have been used to protect low income workers from monopsony conditions.

This vacuum of competition is exactly what has happened in the freelance services industry where two publicly-listed corporate buyers Fiverr and Upwork offering many sellers ostensibly free entry onto their digital platforms have joined forces to buy rankings in sponsored listings from the largest international search engines in order to exercise monopsonist control over the hundreds of thousands of sellers who are in effect buying space on their platforms in return for a commission. Comparable with Coca-Cola Europacific Partners PLC domination of the demand for raw materials and the supply of goods in the European beverage industry, stifling any competitor entering the same labor market, the spending actions of multinationals Fiverr and Upwork have established monopsonist control over freelance talent.

Acting in large part to shield monopsonist gig platforms, from consumer complaints and legal review by employment advocates alike, is the fact governments are doing too little to protect freelancers from being exploited by gig platforms. One of the best examples of this failure is the 2023 Federal court ruling in Australia in the matter of Jamsek v ZG Operations Australia Pty Ltd (No 3) [2023] FCAFC 48 that upheld gig economy workers are "independent contractors" opposed to being employees deserving of job entitlements.

Such court rulings ultimately secure the exploitation of vulnerable workers risking their health in markets where the only space they can earn an increasingly smaller share of consumer spending are the same tightly-controlled platforms. In the Jamsek case the Australian court required two truck drivers Martin Jamsek and Robert Whitby being employed directly by ZG Operations to adduce an exorbitant standard of evidence to prove their employment status. Reversing a previous judgment that held the men were employees, the court held on appeal, "it is not possible to quantify the relevant value of the labor component of the delivery service compared to the other benefits that ZG obtained under the contracts," which in practice put several million freelancers in Australia outside the protection of labor laws there.

Reaction to the Jamsek ruling by Deliveroo, another gig platform exploiting freelance riders in Australia until it failed in massive debt, was reported by the Sydney Morning Herald to one of elation. Deliveroo Australia claimed to have been vindicated from allegations it had sidelined workers rights. By disallowing riders or sellers earning from gig platforms to be classified legally as employees, Deliveroo, like Uber, Fiverr, Upwork et al who all profit from workers' labor through operating monopsonist networks where the only place the worker can earn is by selling in the corporate's network, a anti-competitive zone has become established that will require a major class action on behalf of freelancers on pro bono terms to dislodge in court.

Some of this reasoning can be proven by Priceonomics reports and the fact its data has not been denied by the platforms when challenged is a red flag. The gargantuan flood of information—exabytes of data—overwhelms most data analysts and legal systems and has provided a camouflage or safe harbor for corporate monopsony to the extent the platforms themselves do not need to care about the lack of transparency or defending against similar Jamsek cases for example in a U.S. court.

While all these platforms 'let' a small 1-2% percentage of freelancers on their platforms earn over $100 a month citing Pricenomics data, the majority are not influencers or in strain of to use another example, Emilina Lomas, a Health & Fitness Copywriter from London using Instagram captioning on Fiverr to make thousands per month. With no government action pending and a greater population of freelancers competing for the same business, it has become accepted that gig platforms like Uber exert control over the maximum future earnings of all potential drivers, because individual freelancers cannot win a David vs Goliath battle. Multinational platforms, by walling off the only networks where any freelancer can operate (crushing licensed taxi fare competition in Uber's case) have displaced the traditional contract between freelancer and freelance employer. Whether big business will ever come under enough authoritative scrutiny as employment advocates who question the fairness of gig platforms like multinational Fiverr, Deliveroo and Uber have suggested is beyond the scope of this analysis.

Loss of earnings by freelancers on multinational platforms would continue if it were not for an emerging American 'Tiger economy' of disruptive entrepreneurial ventures currently experiencing rapid economic growth - Wyoming-based HostJane and California-resided Patreon, companies who are improving standards of fairness for freelancers by increasing choice and availability of new audiences of buyers. Like Aldi and Whole Foods' introduction as alternative food retailers unlocked some of Walmart's domination, HostJane, the subject of this inquiry is renewing freedom and flexibility for both consumers to the gig economy by facilitating freelancers to get paid from income sources unavailable through Upwork and Fiverr and unique to the HostJane-Patreon disruption.

HostJane is evidenced to reduce conflicts and increase worker satisfaction, by including on its platform policy incentives to celebrate freelancers as independent contractors who also have a stake in their own business by rewarding those who sell over $5,000 in a month with up to 95% earnings. By reducing freelancer liabilities, and assisting its sellers to capture higher take-home performance based earnings with less taxation, gig work on HostJane is more attractive than working as a freelancer on multinational markertplaces like Upwork where the risks outweigh the cost of entry hurdles for new freelancers with no reviews or work histories on the site.

Today's gig economy is a product of freelancing, which has become an important phenomenon in the human capital market. In the web hosting industry where HostJane has its roots, it is the norm to engage professionals with specific skills as freelancers on a project basis. There is little information available on how hourly-based employees make sense of their relationships with their employers. Professional freelancers are invited to explore on HostJane how to better their relationship with personal clients and start-ups by using a Trello-style board system to facilitate sustainable growth. To arrive at that conclusion this inquiry also examined, as a sub-question, to what extent the identity construction of the professional freelance project team shifted over time, through high work autonomy.

Skilled freelancers seek control, high wages, autonomy and flexibility, and employing firms (before Upwork and Fiverr dominated the market) strived to deliver consistently good quality services to end clients, relying on freelancers. That is the direction HostJane takes its skilled freelancers - as individuals not required to maintain loyalty to their employers. Patreon's business model of subscriptions has also turned that relationship on its head. Whereas a startup, as a newly emerged business venture has 1-5 years on average to develop a viable and financially sustainable business model to meet market needs, the platforms upon which those timespans occur have less time to make an impact than the small businesses they represent. Huge venture capital in the case of Upwork and Fiverr has bridged that gap, rounds of investment that have acted as a stimuli for artificial growth. Research shows that independent work might be viewed as dubious in that there is no business security for sellers on monopsonist platforms doing a disservice to the freelancers they represent.

~ 2 ~

AIRTASKER - A CANARY IN THE COAL MINE

The first comparable marketplace we examined was Airtasker, a Sydney based company. Data were collected from multiple sources, including reviewing relevant tax documents and information, semi-structured interviews, and observations of interactions among professional freelancers on Airtasker. Specialists' commitment contracts showed that around expert consultants had been participated in Airtasker gigs starting from the beginning up of the business and they had been working together for a considerable length of time, fabricating a moderately long haul relationship with Airtasker.

Notwithstanding, in one of the 2023 Airtasker policy reviews after a freelancer was blacklisted by one of the sub-networks that Airtasker subcontracts; it was recorded that a consultant attempted to poach one of Airtasker's principal clients. That consultant was boycotted for rehire.

Aside from that occurrence, end-client assessments and the huge number of rehash gigs demonstrated that consultants who had been working together starting from the beginning up functioned admirably together and delivered great creation results. The absence of educational records likewise demonstrated that these expert specialists were gifted in their particular regions and they could work autonomously with somewhat negligible regulatory help. Email correspondences recorded how a gig creation group functioned.

Specialists went to introductory creation gatherings and got briefings about the particular prerequisites of a specific gig. Whenever specialists had settled on the imaginative bearings with all day regulatory administrators, these consultants worked autonomously. Numerous underlying and various leveled attributes of associations are not material to proficient consultants working for Airtasker. For instance, particularly toward the beginning up stage, consultants didn't typically give progress reports or elect to submit to any assessment cycle. Messages from full-time regulatory staff individuals demonstrated that a few expert specialists loathed examination and observing.

The regional supervisor of Airtasker in Melbourne keeps up with command over consultants' compensation rate and the task of occupations. Monetary archives showed that from its beginning up in 2013 to manageability in 2019, Airtasker's police-checked gig creation business became 500%. Concurring to sequential ATO annual reports, Airtasker figured out how to foster a couple of large corporate clients who were steadfast and connected with Airtasker to rehash yearly reporting. At the point when the business turned practical, gigs with too much scope for a single seller were metered out to an array of different locally based freelancers; the specialists included were paid higher charges than toward the beginning up phase of the business. Exactly the same pattern occurred on Uber where freelancer earnings were docked from 30% to 18% after local competition (in Uber's case taxi firms) were eliminated.

On Airtasker, a task supervisor was likewise added to the full-time managerial group when jobkeeper was announced by the Australian government in 2020, and along with a full-time collaborator, more managerial labor gave backing to gigs. Strategies and methods were additionally refined, with sufficient answers, to guarantee the nature of every gig. In any case, from 2020 to 2023, the venture's revenue compared to investment in freelancer pool indicated an exploitative relationship between freelancers and platform, ending in a website and logo revamp early in February 2023.

Airtasker therefore began the cycle to progress from a turbulent beginning up stage to a more steady and reasonable stage through the improvement of more adhoc clients, upheld by laid out degrees of assets and innovation. Be that as it may, client contracts additionally showed that no steadfast relationship was being created with new clients. New clients created during these two years were one-off clients. As Airtasker gig creation business united and moved into a practical stage, finance reports show that charge installments to proficient creation specialists had likewise expanded.

Airtasker profited from its consultants' solid involvement with no commitment to be faithful to individual freelancers, nor any obligation to improve Airtasker corporate qualities so much as fostering their own standing by means of Airtasker projects. Continuing on toward the feasible development stage, local buyers for example IKEA assembly freelancers, painters and plumbers, evidence showed that as their experience acquired from working with Airtasker made them multi-skilled, flexible, and self-overseeing, their bottom lines did not change. In other words, the profits Airtasker saw by adopting a large scale corporate strategy to freelance marketplaces enriched Airtasker and they have not shared that wealth with their constituent freelancer group.

~ 3 ~

A HOST TURNED MARKETPLACE

Internet outsourcing heralded an open door across lateral free markets for skilled workers who may not be university-educated specialists but who are specialists in the eyes of the buyers who independently employ them to take care of minor tasks for example bug fixing on a website or building a responsive progressive app. Labor that from virtual assistants to music video editors that has always been outsourced as most people do not have the software to fulfil these types of tasks.

The challenge for the marketplace then becomes tied to the efficacy of linking algorithmic skills matching the training and learning opportunities of a pool of freelancers at different educational levels while recruiting freelancers who will be reliable and productive partners in a gig workforce. This is what HostJane has successfully done. Carve out a niche for "Janework" as online freelance jobs are funneled to a small group of "Level 2", "pro" and "rising talent" freelancers on Upwork and Fiverr, HostJane has enabled other freelancers to provide their labor services remotely for clients without exploiting those workers.

A critical value proposition of online labor platforms such as HostJane is matching skilled workers with clients in need of their skills in computer literacy to creative tasks and online lessons. While platforms like eBay rely on reputation feedback from previous buyers, evidence suggests Fiverr and Upwork are essentially ghosting freelancers on their own platforms, particularly those from West African countries like Ghana and Nigeria, who may never get a single order despite having the skills to fulfil demanded tasks.

For those skills that are being improved during freelance work online, respondents reported developing them slightly less frequently than, on average, weekly. Upworkers appear to be more likely to develop their non-cognitive skills to those on PeoplePerHour which recommends Udemy courses to its members, for instance how to communicate with U.S.-based clients to hone their freelancing-specific skills.

In this regard as well as holding a non-discrimatory policy compared with comparable online platforms, HostJane as a workplace focused on serving the needs of small business VPS clients, encourages individual learning activities as part of the way the platform has been designed to crowdfund talent; designing complex interdependencies inherent in organizational work to flourish. Overall, HostJane freelancers' learning strategies appear to consist mainly of on-the-job learning without relying on any rote learning or educational program of (self-serving) formal goal-setting or learning plans commonplace within the large multinational platforms like Fiverr.

The improvement of WiFi and broadband internet in developing countries has brought more educated freelancers to HostJane as an online learning provider that allows migrants and even refugees with skills to enter a market receptive to talent on the basis of merit, not nationality or IP geolocation.

~ 4 ~

REFERENCES

M. Ameri, S. Rogers, L. Schur, and D. Kruse, "No room at the inn? disability access in the new sharing economy," Academy of Management Discoveries, vol. 6, no. 2, pp. 176–205, 2020.

Lehdonvirta, V. et al. (2019). The global platform economy: a new offshoring institution enabling emerging-economy microproviders. Journal of management, Vol. 45, No 2, pp. 567-599.

Pallais, A. (2014). Inefficient hiring in entry-level labor markets. American economic review, Vol. 104, No 11, pp. 3565-3599.

Parker, G, van Alstyne, M., & Choudary, S. 2016, 'Platform Revolution: How Networked Markets Are Transforming the Economy – And How to Make Them Work for You'. W. W. Norton & Company Ltd, New York.

Gomez-Herrera, E; Mueller-Langer, F. (2019). Is there a gender wage gap in online labor markets? Evidence from over 250000 projects and 2.5 million wage bill proposals. JRC digital economy working paper 2019-01

R. Rosario and G. Widmeyer, "An exploratory review of design principles in constructivist gaming learning environments," Journal of Information Systems Education, vol. 20, no. 3, pp. 289–300, 2016

Kenney Martin, Zysman John, 2016. 'The Rise of the Platform Economy. Issues in Science and technology.' Volume XXXII Issue 3, Spring 2016.

Boudreau, Kevin J., and Andrei Hagiu 2009. "Platform Rules: Multi-Sided Platforms As Regulators." In Platforms, Markets and Innovation, edited by Annabelle Gawer. Cheltenham, UK: Edward Elgar Publishing, 2009.

E. Ert and A. Fleischer, "The evolution of trust in Airbnb: A case of home rental," Annals of Tourism Research, vol. 75, pp. 279–287, 2019.

F. Hawlitschek, B. Notheisen, and T. Teubner, "The limits of trust-free systems: A literature review on blockchain technology and trust in the sharing economy," Electronic Commerce Research and Applications, vol. 29, pp. 50–63, 2018.

Ghazawneh, A. & Mansour, O. (2015), Value Creation in Digital Marketplaces: Developers Perspective, Thirty Sixth International Conference on Information Systems, Fort Worth 2015.

www.ingramcontent.com/pod-product-compliance
Lightning Source LLC
LaVergne TN
LVHW021051100526
838202LV00082B/5460